Follow me on twitter

@fabulousmar

#SANDYCOMEATME

A Nightmare Documented-Sandy Storm 2012

"By"

Marlene Paulin

Table of Contents

Introduction

Angela Rose Dresch is a Thirteen-year-old girl that lives near the Tottenville beach in N.Y. with her mother Patricia and her father George. Angela is happy and healthy, preparing to graduate eighth grade and start high school. She loves Instagram, Facebook and just got a boyfriend. She has tons of friends. She dreams of becoming a Veterinarian someday. She wants a cute cupcake dress for Prom. Angela also wants to get married someday and have a family. How would she ever know that she would never even make it to her fourteenth birthday?

My name is Marlene; I am not just praising a hero or ridiculing an opinion, just speaking the truth. The truth hurts sometimes or brings laughter, sorrow, or tears. I speak it anyway. I want the world to know Sandy showed no mercy. She stole some people we loved very much.

This book is for Angela wherever you are we love you and miss you so much.

Chapter 1

Setting the Scene

August 20th of 2011

"This will be the storm of the century", everyone was told to prepare him or herself. Where have we heard this before? The meteorologists have said this before many times over the past 30 years. The Storm was rolling in and the Dresch family was being evacuated because a category three hurricane Irene. She had torn through the Bahamas and left the Caribbean in shambles. "The storm is on its way to NY and people must prepare for the worst" the news was saying. Everyone is told to buy necessities, and water bottles. New York and New Jersey was evacuating all homes that are within a mile of the shore and ocean front homes. "It will be devastating" was all the media kept saying .The stores were mobbed with people stocking up on supplies and lanterns and matches, flashlights, water bottles, candles, and canned foods were just flying off the shelves. "Do we really have to do this? I mean seriously... weather forecasts are always so wrong!" I had complained, "Really you can stick your head out the window and find out the weather forecast!" That is what my mom always says. I love a sense of humor and simple logic that is my mom. It seems that common sense is a super power her and I possess.

Patricia, George, and Angela Dresch are my family from my first marriage to Gerard, Patricia's brother. They took the predictions seriously. They followed this normal procedure after 20 years of living so close to the ocean. Over the last 10 years instead of just having water in the basement, it seemed to rise up a little bit further every year. There seemed to be signs that the storms were becoming somewhat more severe in hindsight. There were signs of progressive intensity. There were not enough signs to have given them the slightest inkling that things were changing as much as they were. There would be storms so drastic that we have never seen anything like it. Storms changing so much so, setting the scene for "Sandy". The changing science of weather and the events in summer of 2011 sealed the fate of the the Dresch family and their decisions.

Being that we live close to the ocean about seven minutes inland, we are always cautioned of severe weather if we are in the path of tropical storms but there were never hurricane threats. I have never taken any storm threats very seriously. "New Jersey does not ever have any weather that is life-threatening." was what I was told and that is what I believed. There were never any narrow escapes or scares. My family (My husband Michael, myself, my two teen daughters Miquela and

Marielle and my youngest daughter Mariah just 7 months old at the time of Irene) live a few miles from Point Pleasant beach so we were not at all worried. Our neighborhood was not evacuated either and we were doubting the severity. We stocked up anyway and waited for the storm. My oldest daughter Miquela was talking to her cousin Angela and she told her that they were leaving. They had been evacuated because Irene was coming.

As I was saying, the Dresch family was very familiar with the process because they have been living on that street and all of these years, being evacuated was not such a surprise. There was one house between them and the ocean. As per the course of action Patricia, George and their daughter Angela left their home. They stayed in the house next to their church where Patricia works. When Irene was said to hit and as the evening came and the hype lessened, it was quite apparent that the storm of the century was just rain and a little wind. However, Patricia and George were still glad they took all precautions that is until they returned to their home.

The next morning they went back to their house and discovered that thieves took full advantage of the empty homes on their street, Yetman Avenue. The Dresch's were looted. The men who robbed hundreds of dollars worth of tools from their garage were caught but only one was convicted. George was infuriated. They left to be safe and left their home vulnerable. As usual, the meteorologist's predictions were inaccurate and they had evacuated for no reason. As a result, they were robbed. The family wondered is it worth it? It turns out, each time they evacuated they returned home and there was never any more than a little water in the basement. Was it worth packing up? Leaving their home, and now being robbed? I guess most people would say no, but you might change your mind after you read the rest of this story.

I can only tell the story and its details from where I sit. Fortunately, I am front and center, but for the most part Unaffected. Let me go back to the beginning, introduce myself, and explain how I fit into this tragedy.

I have known Patricia and George for 20 years, you see I was married to Patricia's brother Gerard for 7 years we have two daughters together Miquela and Marielle and we were together for 10 years. About the time, Gerard and I hit our rough road in the marriage, and in late spring of 1999, Patricia and George had their second daughter Angela Rose. She was born on April 30, 1999 my daughters were just 2 years old and 6 months old and over the divorce and the next thirteen years, the three girls were inseparable. Marielle tends to be a little over whelming and she may hog or take over a person. She Demands their attention but it seemed that Angela, knowing them both all her short life, knew exactly how to deal with them both and keep their friendships between the three of them close and happy even though three is a hard number to deal with.

My ex husband Gerard would pick up Angela and bring her wherever they were going, and usually just to go to his apartment and let them have a sleepover just for them to have company and entertain each other. Angela is always there and included with the girls and their weekend plans. When Gerard and his girlfriend Vicki were going out, Patricia always had the girls stay there with them. They went on vacations and spent all the holidays together. If the girls were not with me, they were with Gerard, Patricia, and George also, of course, Angela.

Jo Ann Gerard, Angela, Marielle, Miquela and Patricia

As the years went on, they became very close talking on facetime, texting, and constantly communicating. They are teenagers now so have their own laptops and cell phones. Once Marielle was on facetime with Angela and I didn't know it. Sometimes they wouldn't even talk! She was home alone after school because Patricia was working, so I guess it felt like she had company being connected to Marielle or Miquela. I sat down to dinner and then realized we were plus one! Angela just started talking and that's when I knew that she was streaming live on facetime. We all laughed. Of course, that was preceded with Marielle showing her the food in her mouth.

Even when they were not together on the weekends, Angela's name was spoken every day the last thirteen years but I never gave it a second thought until now that she is gone.

I re-married and had my third daughter Mariah Ashley born on 1/11/11 and by now the girls have Angela come and stay over with us on Easter break and in the summer. Angela considers Mariah her baby cousin, and does not understand or care that there is a disconnection. I told the girls "people don't divorce kids, and I still love Angela and consider her my niece". She is welcome anytime in my home. Besides, she is very quiet and with the new baby in the house that is very important to me! The bond was not just cousins it was like a sister relationship between the three of them and now add baby Mariah in the mix for good measure and they are cousins and best friends for life.

She was just there, just one of us, never any
uncomfortable feelings she was sweet, polite and timid.
Someone you can be yourself around. Angela was not
someone you can get mad at or sick of, she just went with
the flow. Angela was just an all-around great kid.

Pictured here is Angela, reading a book to Mariah in the summer of 2011 several weeks after the storm Irene.

Angela loved Ice-skating, right before summer started she fell while skating and broke her arm, and she was planning to ask for her own skates for Christmas she wanted them so badly she was talking about it in the summer! Sadly, Christmas never came for her.

Early September 2011, my girls started talking to me about "The Iconic Boys" I did not know it at the time but, they turned out to be significant in the days following Sandy. Miquela had explained to me how the iconic boys had been on season 6 of the TV show America's Best Dance Crew. Miquela is a dancer and this did not surprise me that she was interested in Boys that danced. I said to her, "Who is this now?" being The Jonas Brothers and the Naked Brothers Band came in and out of the scene so quickly. I certainly did not take any of their fads and crushes very seriously.

"Angela likes them and she showed us videos of them dancing and now we like them, they are a dance group they are having a meet and greet, can you PLEASE, take us and Angela and Kat to the Roller Jam on Staten

Island?" Miquela always rambles on and begged me because she knows that I usually give in to these whims. She knew that Patricia could not drive and Gerard was working, I was their only hope for this venture. I did try to get out of it because it is a 45-minute ride to the house and I do not have room in my car for everyone. But I gave in, I figured why not , make them happy, the summer was just about over and being I had the baby we didn't do all that much. We headed out on our way to the house. Angela and her friend Katherine Hrzic, better known as "Kat" were there ready outside and waiting anxiously. Then they all squished in and I took a picture. When I dropped them off, I snapped a few more pictures and noticed the line wrapped around the building! Luckily, it was a nice day, because they waited six hours on line to finally meet these kids. "Are you guys kidding me? Do you really want to wait on this line? This is crazy!" I said "Are you sure you want me to leave you here you're going to be waiting outside for a very long time, and Daddy is definitely coming here?" I asked the girls, and Marielle said, "It's not daddy that is picking us up, Uncle George is getting us after work."

Uncle George got them that evening. Gerard picked them up after that. "I still can't believe we met them," Miquela said it as if it they were superstars, who knows maybe someday they will be.

The families work together thank god, for the kids. Back in July Angela had stayed with us for four days through our fourth of July BBQ and entertained the girls for me for a few days and I had become close with her, before this we hadn't had very much of a relationship because of the divorce. I had listened to the girls tell stories about her and describe what kind of person she is. They would talk about what she did and things she said, but did not get to spend time with her until recently. I am so glad that Patricia started allowing her to stay here and I got the opportunity to know her. It also gave my husband Michael an opportunity to know her, the last time she stayed with us he took them to Great Adventure. Therefore, I guess what I am trying to say, is that by now not only did Miquela and Marielle know and love Angela, but so did we. By the time the nightmare of Sandy Storm 2012 hit, Angela was like one of the family members here, as well as with her family at home. In the pages ahead, I will relive the horror and the tragic events as they unfolded.

Chapter 2

Storm Preparation

Friday, October 26, 2012

The forecast was saying that on Sunday, October 28 2012 the "Storm of the Century" was to hit… again. Although this storm was to be different from the other storms, this storm was going to tear up the coastline in NY and NJ. Some people doubted the prediction. Is it any wonder that some might not take the warnings very seriously? There were so many false alarms. Although, there where some that the prediction seemed to send them into a frenzy. Everyone panicked and bought stores out of water bottles and camping gear. You would think it was the end of the world.

"They said on the news that we might lose power for a few days." My husband informed me. "Really?" I asked He Said "Yeah but you know how they hype it up, maybe they are trying to boost the economy", and he gave me a half smile … "all those lanterns, generators, and flashlights. They scare the shit out of people." Michael has a way with words. Our conversation lagged and I really did not give it a second thought. I had stocked up and got gas, everything was as it should be. I sent text back and forth to my friend Ross in Florida. I had deemed him "Weather boy" because he was always talking weather, and told him he should be ashamed. He was such a slacker because he did not inform me of a hurricane that was to hit our area in just a few days, the Storm they are calling Sandy. He gave me Kudos for beating him to the punch on this information then he sent a snap shot of his TV news channel. It was clearly showing this turmoil headed straight for us, like a nefarious perpetrator stalking a victim. I have to admit my jaw dropped, it was very scary and it made me stop and think but, I was still not convinced. Little did I know Sandy was ruthless and unstoppable!

I drove the girls to the dollar store the next day, "We need to get Arizona teas and snacks if there's a storm coming!" Marielle said, she said it as if that was the most important thing in the world. I grabbed a small purple flashlight while I was there. I did not know it at the time but that flashlight would be my best friend for six days. I also filled my tank with gas and grabbed a case of water bottles because everyone was. School was canceled because of the impending threat but, still it had not dawned on me or anyone I spoke to that the meteorologists may be right on with their prediction of this storm.

"Ok, I guess we're all prepared" I said. I thought it would probably blow over. However, in reality NOTHING could have prepared us for the days to come.

I heard the girls chatter with friends and their cousin Angela, they had told me, that Angela, Aunt Patricia and Uncle George were evacuated from the house again, as usual but this time they are not leaving. Angela told Miquela that Aunt Patricia said 'we can live in the car if we have to'. They were not taking it seriously, almost joking about the forecast.

Gerard had told me that George decided to move their cars a few blocks away, so they would be safe from water damage. I don't think too many people really expected this storm to be as catastrophic as it would wind up being and certainly not Patricia and George who thought to keep the cars safe , but not themselves. I texted my friend Cathy McNaboe who lives right on the water in

Bayville N.J. As the rain got heavier and the wind picked up, we still had partial power. It was approximately 3pm on Sunday October 28th when Cathy called and said, "How are you guys doing?" She also added "just lost power about an hour ago" I had told her that we still had some and it was like a brown out with dim lights, very creepy. She also explained to me that they were urged to evacuate but did not leave. I thought to myself geez not another one that was supposed to leave and did not.

Shorty after our power went totally out, approximately 3:00pm on Sunday. It was just somewhat exciting at this point, we had candles lit and my husband was returning from work. I had gotten the baby to bed with a few flash lights as night lights and the 80 mile an hour winds whipped through the town, curious to experience this phenomenon, all four of us stood out on our 5ft by 4ft front stoop feeling daring and scared but in awe of the crazy storm. "This is just nuts" I said,

"I have never seen anything like this in all my years, it's just crazy!" Sandy was like nothing any of us had ever seen. You could not stand out there for long because there were sticks and leaves blowing in the wind whipping in all directions. It was a very scary, ominous feeling. There was just total blackness. The trees were bending. Suddenly, the transformer that is located directly behind our house made a loud noise, and a blue light lit up the sky for just a second. This made everything seem more real. I started thinking the forecast was very accurate. It was a natural disaster so out of control. Sandy cannot be stopped. She cannot be arrested by the law or stopped by a threat. Sandy cannot be shot or obtained by the government… Even scarier than terrorists, or pure evil that can be punished or stopped. Nature is ferocious, much more savage than humans can absorb. Sandy's obscure approach left everyone, including us, perplexed. What do we do?

What will we need? How can we protect ourselves? Being we did not have TV and no lights or power to charge our phones we all went to bed relatively early.

The next morning the temperature was dropping and I hated to be making Mariah uncomfortable she seemed scared when she woke up and it was unusually cold, dark, and quiet and she could not watch Sesame Street as she usually would. These things seem to very important to me at the time. I believe that priorities shift when a tragedy strikes in a new perspective your life changes forever.

By 9:00am I got text from my Ex husband Gerard that he spoke to Patricia around 7:30pm during the storm and the addition to the house they built, had been washed away in the storm and he said, "I called 911, I was on hold for an hour." Gerard told me but he did not sleep that night until he got through. He had to let them know that Patricia, George, and Angela were left stranded at the end of Yetman Avenue. "I haven't been able to reach them," Gerard explained, "they told me that the water was rising and they were up stairs" his voice was panicked.

Patricia said, "Its too late, the water was rising to the upstairs window!" He told me they had a lot of water in the house. He kept telling them to get out however she said they could not. Patricia believed the water was rising too fast…. I was so worried when I heard this. I kept thinking to myself, why would they stay? How do you stay in the house filling up with water? Why not try to swim to safety? It just seemed like there were so many other options. This was so preventable. Common sense would tell you if the attachment of the house washed away then it might happen to the rest of it! If the foundation of the house was underwater, destroyed and unstable then how can it hold up the rest of the house? I was still not thinking of the worst possible scenario. I presumed that they were stranded. I believed that they would lose their belongings because of water damage. I never thought the worst would happen. Things like that you never believe will happen to you or your family. You never think that something so horrific may be your reality.

I realized in the morning light that Sandy wreaked havoc nothing but a trail of destruction in her path. I had no Idea yet how devastating the outcome would be. Everyone in our house was awake by now. We had a pathetic excuse for coffee with my resourceful boiled water and filters. We were having some breakfast. Then the girls and I were planning on going to the car to waste gas and charge our phones when I received the most disturbing phone call of my life.

Chapter 3

Havoc

No "Hello" or prelude just Gerard in a panic, "Angela and George are missing" the fear in his voice was indescribable. My whole body went cold and my hands shook uncontrollable "OH MY GOD, OH MY GOD" was all I could find to say. The girls stopped in their tracks waiting to hear more of what I might say. Michael looked at me aggravated and said what happened? As though I should move the phone and tell him immediately. I could barely breathe, I could not even speak I just kept listening.

"Patricia is in the hospital, the entire house is gone. I'm driving there now to see what's going on but I can't get there because the Verrazano Bridge is closed..." Gerard had explained to me "I have been here for two hours on the Parkway, and it is not open yet" he had no choice but to wait. Just then, my phone cut out "Hello? Gerard are you there?" OH MY GOD! I had to go tell the girls they had gone to their room. "That was daddy he said Angela and Uncle George are missing." All I could do to try to cover my panic was to put my hand over my mouth. I was shaking my head in utter disbelief. I was shaking and I knew what the out come might be. They did not grasp the concept and I was not ready to tell them. What goes through your head? How do I tell my girls that their cousin and best friend that they spend their weekends with since they were born was killed in this horrific storm? I had to tell them that their uncle might also have been killed. How do they deal with that at their age? How can I help them deal with that? I was so shaken myself from the news that I did not know who to turn to. I did not know who to talk to or how to talk to them.

They back room of the house is gone washed away

They back room of the house is gone washed away

That's FKN nuts. And are they ok???

Oct 29, 2012, 9:19 PM

13 houses in Brick are on Fire

They were on 2nd floor last I spoke

 Text Message Send

I held out hope that this was all just a scary mistake. I was hoping that they went into the hospital separately. I hoped we would sigh a big sigh of relief and laugh about the scare. When I told the girls, they did not know what to think and did not know how to react. All I can think of is they have no idea what I am saying. There is no set way to deal with things that come your way but as a mother, you think, "How can I explain this?" On the other hand, "How do I fix this?" I tried to call Gerard back but I could not get through. My phone was not able to dial out. There were no cell towers working in Brick. It felt like the end of the world. I tried to call my mom to see if they were ok and could not get through. Sandy hit Bricktown and Point Pleasant very badly. Sadly, the outcome was not as I had hoped. I had gotten a brief voicemail from Gerard and he just said, "Call me back" I had heard the grief and pain in his voice. I knew that Angela had died. It is much worse than anyone would imagine. Angela Rose Dresch 13 years old had drowned in the wake of super storms Sandy 2012. Gerard identified her body... he sent me the voice mail to call him back and I could hear the pain in his voice. His heart was breaking. He could barely get the words out. I did not need to call back to know what had happened. The body of the young girl that was brought

into the hospital with Patricia was in fact Angela.

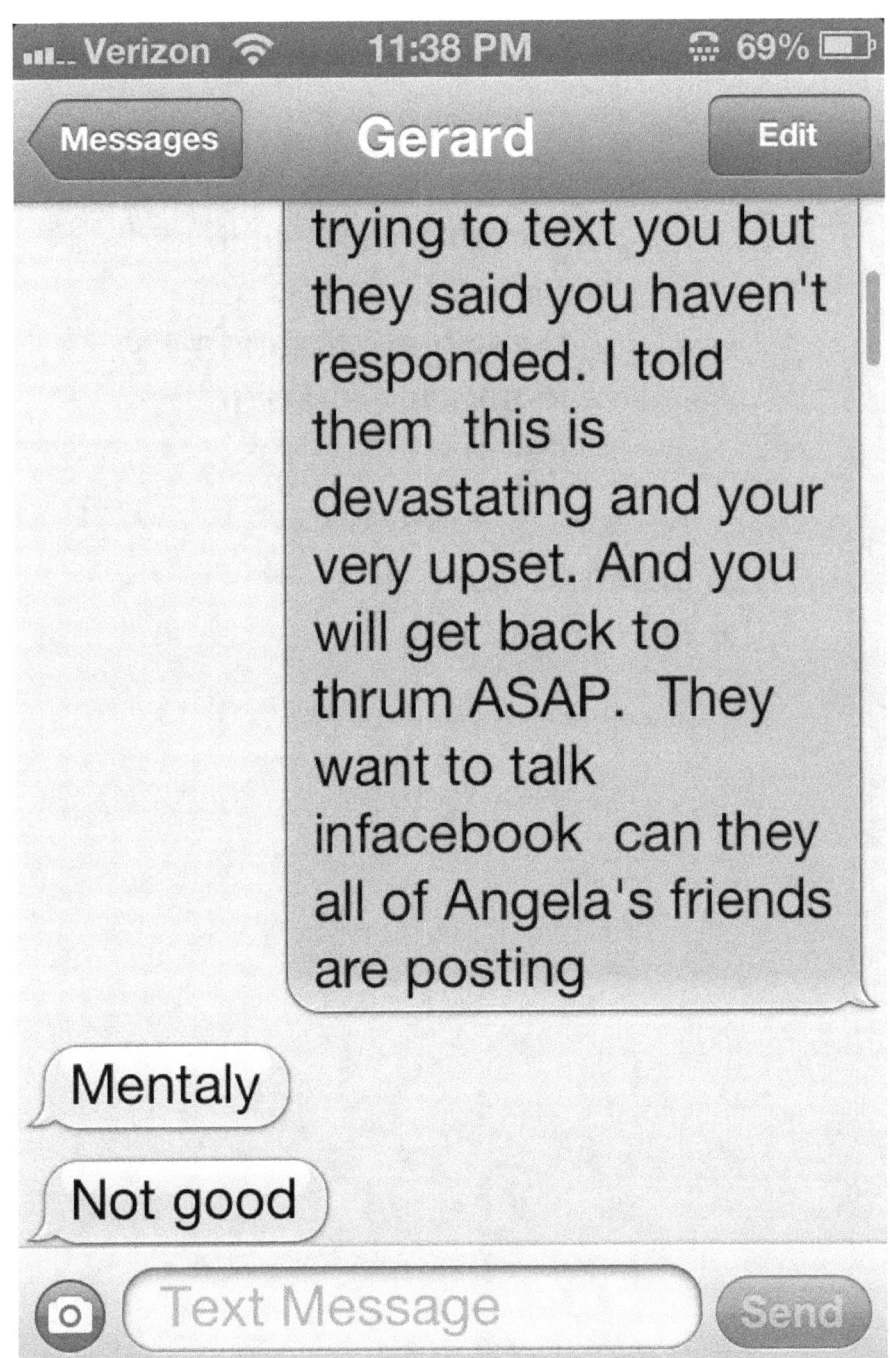

trying to text you but they said you haven't responded. I told them this is devastating and your very upset. And you will get back to thrum ASAP. They want to talk infacebook can they all of Angela's friends are posting

Mentaly

Not good

Text Message

Send

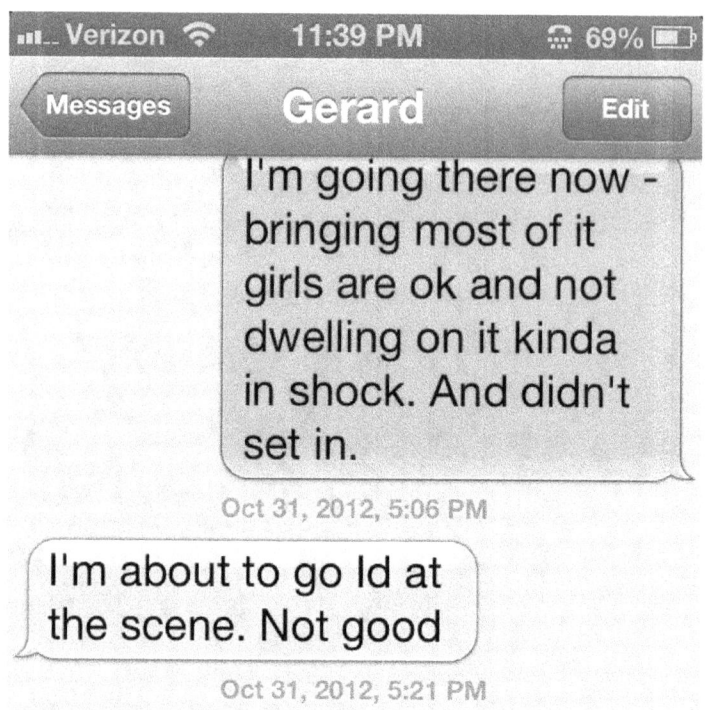

I'm going there now -
bringing most of it
girls are ok and not
dwelling on it kinda
in shock. And didn't
set in.

Oct 31, 2012, 5:06 PM

I'm about to go Id at
the scene. Not good

Oct 31, 2012, 5:21 PM

you

Oct 31, 2012, 6:24 PM

It was him

Oh no omg this is horrible

Patrica uh. Hang in there

I'm here they just told her.This is the most horrific thing

OMG. Call me when you can omg

Oct 31, 2012, 7:26 PM

Text Message   Send

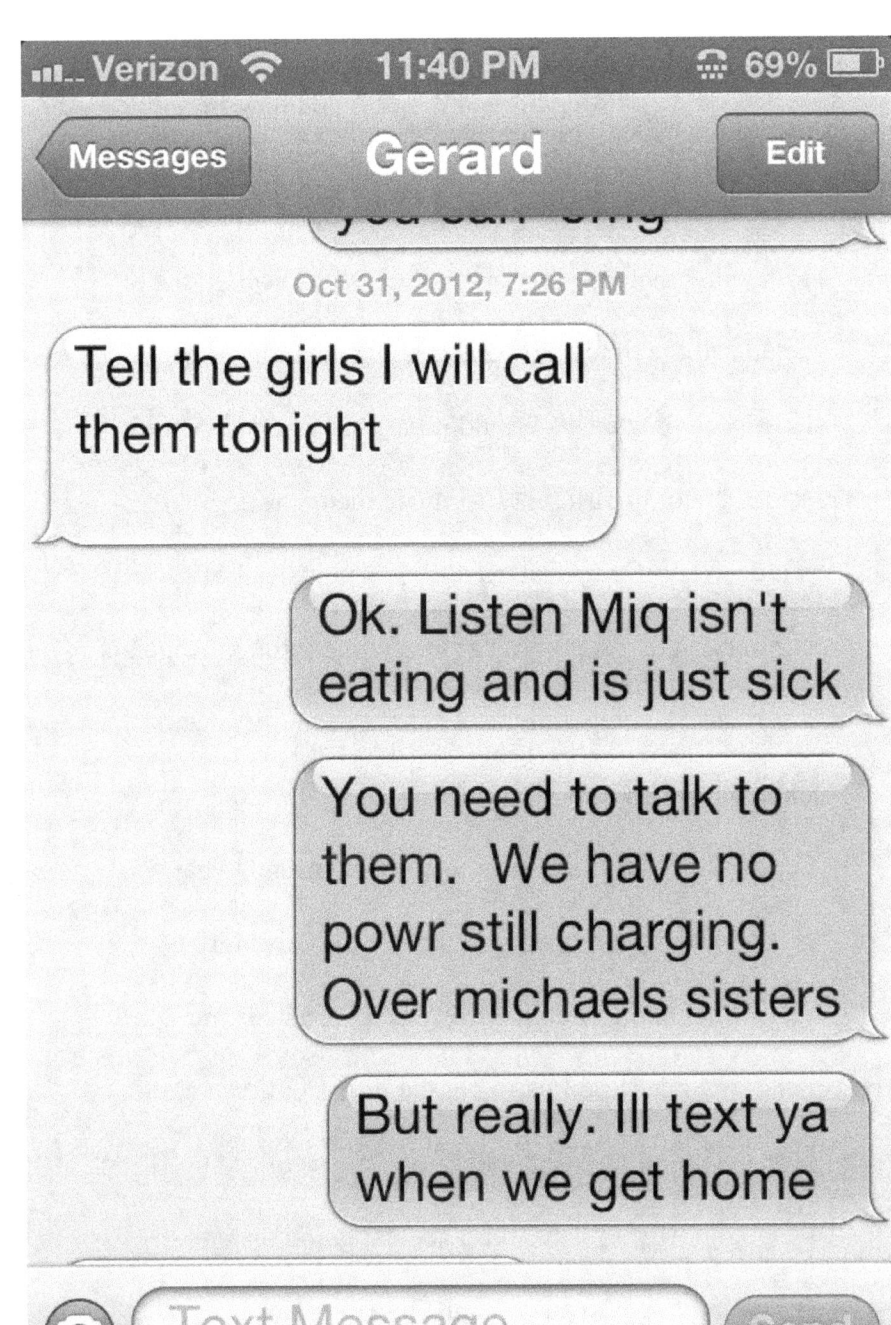

Oct 31, 2012, 7:26 PM

Tell the girls I will call them tonight

Ok. Listen Miq isn't eating and is just sick

You need to talk to them. We have no powr still charging. Over michaels sisters

But really. Ill text ya when we get home

Text Message Send

This is the kind of thing that affects you the rest of your life. You go over the conversation repeatedly in your mind and the emotions keep coming back. It is something that happens that makes you reflect on the details all the time and wonder how could this tragedy have been prevented. Would it have mattered if Gerard said something different that made them change their mind? What if they just tried to get out instead of climbing up the stairs? What was going through Angela's head those last few minutes I cannot even imagine. At that point, she knew all of her belongings were underwater. The water was so cold and rough, what was going through her mind right before the wave hit? I picture her and I imagine being there. It haunts me. I see her in my head and I can't get the image out. She could hear the house creaking and knew it was collapsing. Then the cold powerful wave hit. I see her going under struggling to get to air. It is just horrible. I wonder what

George was thinking at the end. It must have been torture to see your family in that situation. He must have felt so sorry for staying at the house. The man that everyone went to for help spent the last minutes of his life completely helpless.

Patricia was trying to save Angela. They were both so scared. Patricia and George knew that they put her in that position. I can imagine myself making that decision and then wishing I had not. The whole thing is such a travesty.

You spend so much of your precious time wasting your thoughts your money and your life and time on things that really do not matter. A person that values their possessions excessively and collects things just does not make sense to me. I guess all is okay as long as you remember you cannot take it with you and enjoy your life. However, possessions are not what matters in the end. Only the love and kindness matters. Sometimes it takes a tragedy in someone else's life to make you realize what is irreplaceable in your own life. I am so much more able to be present and enjoy my daughters now. I think about Patricia everyday and the fact that she does not have one of her daughters anymore due to her and her husbands' bad decision. Catastrophic perfect storm "Sandy 2012" left us with a story that is so heart wrenching it is not easily forgotten. Every decision has a consequence and every action has an equal and opposite reaction. I am sure the thought of her choice and what happened must go through Patricia's head so many times every day. I think for her it is probably more difficult that she lived through all this. She was left stranded in the wreckage and it must have been an angel that saved her from death. She must have more to do here in this world. She has to start life over. Surviving Sandy is only half the battle for her. She is starting over now after losing

George and Angela. She is trying to rebuild her life.

Thankfully, she has her faith in God, her extended family,

and the kindness of strangers. She is fortunate that so

many people heard her story and they started to help.

Chapter 4

Repercussions and Premonitions

Other than losing power, my home stayed intact. Many

homes in Brick N.J. had burned because of gas leaks. In

fact, sixty-three homes in Brick about ten minutes from my

house on the shoreline and over a hundred in Queens N.Y.

that burned uncontrollably. In an article in The New York

Times on November 17th 2012, it stated that the total death

toll from Sandy had reached 109 people. Whenever I would

think about my retirement, I would see this vision of me but

it is always the view from behind. I see the back of my

head. I see myself looking out into the ocean my home is

on the Waterfront. I have always believed I would have an

oceanfront home with the patio and sliding glass doors that

leads to the ocean. I have dreamed of this home, I have

never seen myself from the front. I am wearing a white

sweater and I'm guessing I am old. I wonder if this was a premonition of this book, or this event, or an actual premonition of me living there. Maybe it was just a dream. I wonder if it will happen in reality, after this I do not think I will be able to buy a home on the water.

The thought of the cold, dark, or the ocean brings me back to that night and this horrific event. It reminds me of the storm and of course Angela.

I went to my car, charged my phone, and called my friend Heather Borkowski. I realize that I could not get through. Brick town was hit hard I could not make outgoing calls. I tried again and now somehow it got through to her voxer, which is an app. I told her I cannot call but I can receive calls.

Heather and my parent's live North of Brick. Mom and Dads house is in the Woodbridge area. They did not lose power for very long and the cell towers were only affected for a few hours as well. I told her to please tell

my parents that - temporarily Brick had no cell service. I

could only except calls but could not call them. Even

some incoming calls were going right to voicemail. She

called them for me and verified they were safe. Then I

told Heather of the horrible tragedy. Her reaction was just

complete shock. She said how sorry she was. I knew

when I started talking that it is usually impossible to find

the right words when you hear news like this but, Heather

always makes me feel like she is there for me and

understands. If I cannot talk to my mom, she is the person

I turn to. I was so thankful to speak to her finally with all

this going on. When Gerard called about Angela and I

could not call out, I completely freaked that I couldn't tell

her and originally he only said, "There was a young

female body brought in to the hospital with Patricia, they

think its Angela. I have to go ID the body." I cannot

imagine doing that. My family is quite lucky. We have

been free from tragedy and fatal accidents with one exception.

It was so difficult for me through all this, not being able to call my mom. Not being in touch with my family to let them know what was going on. I had to deal with all this pain, grief, disarray and uncertainty alone. Michael is a good man but he has a hard time being supportive emotionally unfortunately. The girls were very distant. I just felt forgotten. Lost and alone like the unacknowledged griever. Almost like a messenger.

A short while later I got the call that I dreaded, " its her" he said sobbing " Its her ,she's gone" and he yelled something but It wasn't audible. Then more sobbing he said, "Jo Ann is calling in and I can not talk to her, I can't answer. This cannot be happening, it's just a horrific nightmare!" he yelled! Then he concluded with "I have to go", as he sobbed and he hung up.

Information like this is something that kind of lays on top you know? Something you do not want to believe so you doubt it was the right information. I was in the car, and I choked up, my eyes filled with tears I took a few long slow deep breaths. You can do this I thought to myself. The girls did not have much reaction when I informed them they were missing I am sure it was shock and numbness. I took more deep breaths. I walked in and just shook my head no and said, "It was her, that was Daddy on the phone and he said it was Angela."

It was later that Gerard had composed himself and called back after speaking to Patricia. Now the horror that only lived in her and Gerard also lives in me. He said, "She remembers every detail now I can't get this nightmare out of my head." Gerard continued, "After the addition fell off and washed away the water started filling up the downstairs of the house, they went up stairs to the bathroom." Patricia had told Gerard that Angela was so scared and that they heard the walls and floors caving in. The water was rising fast. The water quickly rose up the stairs and kept rising and soon it was up to their necks. Angela was petrified. He had recapped everything to me in disbelief while trying to deal with his own grief. The perfect storm was aligned with the exact time of the full moon at 7:50pm and the repercussions were ferocious. The wave was approximately thirty-feet high and crashed onto the house and she had held Angela by her arm tightly. This was the end. The small house was no match for this force of nature.

The creeks got louder the floor gave out as the roof fell and hit Patricia and she lost her grip on Angela. That was the last time she saw her alive. Patricia said she suddenly was in the backyard she grabbed hold of her bathroom wall she recognized the soap dish holder and heard George screaming for help, but she was helpless. Patricia called out for Angela but there was no reply."

Patricia would remain stranded in the cold water for over five hours and she used the phone wires to move herself along and stay afloat then finally climbed onto someone's deck that was detached and floating a few blocks away. The water was approximately thirty feet high, judging from the height of the telephone poles and the debris was everywhere. She said later to my daughter Miquela that she could see someone's roof floating and spinning in a circle…..and she prayed. Patricia was rescued because of Gerard's call to 911. No one knew they were out there but the call got through and Fire fighters were sent to Yetman Avenue. Many of them were on the scene for many hours that night but there was one fire fighter in particular his name is Marc Thalheimer. Gerard spoke with him and he explained that he had seen from the corner of his eye a light in the far distance. It was dim, and probably about a mile away in the pitch black but it lead him to the area where Patricia was. She floated on the deck it like a raft until the water was gone, and the tide went back out. When he got to her, she was shielding herself from the rain in a pile of debris. She collapsed into his arms. It was then that Patricia knew she finally was headed for safety. She had been out there for over five hours in the ice-cold water. She also said she did not have a flashlight.

This was one of the first articles I saw including this before and after picture and the announcement that it had been Angela's body that was found .A graphic before and after picture of the house .The small house next to Patricia's was also gone but, fortunately they had evacuated. I get an eerie feeling looking at this picture. I look at the picture of the house and I can remember my arms filled with bags, presents, and kids while George tried to hold the door for me being a wise guy of course and everyone was always laughing. They were a loud Italian family that I had married into. There were beautiful Christmas decorations everywhere, dishes with candy, and gifts piled high. I see flashes of pictures and people and of days gone by, time spent with Gerard's family.

 Then the after picture is just a horrific scene. I got tears in my eyes it was so scary. All that remains of their home are those stairs. This article was printed on October 29th 2012 and was published before they found and identified George.

13-year-old Angela Dresch is ID'd as Staten Island victim of Hurricane Sandy

Mark D. Stein/Staten Island Advance
10/30/2012 2:49 PM

Patricia spent 5 days in the hospital after the water came through and tore this family apart. The house had literally collapsed on her. When she was admitted into the hospital, her body temperature was 81 degrees and that is considered severe hypothermia (68-82 degrees). Doctors said no one survives that, it is a miracle she is alive to tell the horror of that evening.

This photo is of the search team looking for George. They

had closed off six blocks in the area to search.

Gerard had told me how horrible it was that they had to tell Patricia that her daughter was found dead. My heart aches for her. It was not until two days later that Georges body was found on Halloween 2012. Gerard had told me that George's body was not in very good shape and he did not look like himself. He had been tossed around for two days in the water and debris. On Halloween night, we were over my husbands sister's house charging our phones and washing our hair, enjoying the heat and electricity that we so desperately missed when I got the call from Gerard. He had gone and positively identified the body of George Dresch, Angela's father. I cannot imagine how hard that must have been to have to go and identify a second family member. Gerard was the only one left. His older sister Carol Ann passed away June 26th 2002 from ovarian cancer. His father had passed away from an aneurysm in his abdomen that had become infected. November 8th 2006 his mom just died recently in May of 2012 may she had Alzheimer's and dementia but died peacefully from old age. However, this being said there was no one else to ID the body's .Gerard told me "this is what my dad would've been doing, this was his job but now he's gone and I have to do it." He felt the burden and responsibility to take over and take care of his sister the way his dad would have.

During all the craziness, I busted out the only Christmas presents I had bought so far and gave them to everyone. I bought my husband and myself and all three daughters infinity bracelets. I handed them out. Miquela and Marielle both said to me that Angela loved the infinity sign. I had no Idea and I usually do not give Christmas gifts in October. Hummmm Coincidence, maybe, but who knows why we do the things we do, or make the decisions we make. Maybe Angel Angela told me to give the bracelets out.

The word got out about this devastating tragedy and the posts and tweets poured through the social media. Facebook was flooded with post from Angela's friends and classmates. Pictures of her surfaced everywhere there was even one estranged relative from George's side of the family who decided to join the cause and chime in with everyone else about missing Angela (whom she had never met) and her uncle George. Ironically, I knew that Patricia and George did not spend any time with any of George's family and it seemed this girl was simply looking for attention. People came out of the woodwork. A friend of my daughters heard the story and her cousin Lisa just so happened to work for the Katie Couric Show on ABC channel 7 she was in charge of organizing the shows segments and she had contacted me. The girls name was Lisa. She asked if the girls could be interviewed for the show. Gerard did not want to do it and he did not think it was a good idea but I talked him into it. I told him it would be good to get donations and then he agreed and went to open an account for the donations. After he checked with Jo Ann they checked with Patricia and we got the ok, I told her the girls would be able to talk to her.

On day six after Sandy very early I got a call from Lisa telling me I need to get the girls there myself for the interview. It was because you see the gas lines were extremely long, and it snowed. The waiting time was about three hours to get your tank filled with gas. I just knew I had to get them there for some reason. Maybe I had to get there myself for peace of mind or just to see the site or maybe for this book.

The distance from brick to Staten Island I suppose was a little too far for the limousine to come and get us considering the weather. The snow and being the distance, they could not get a car to us. I knew I had to get the girls there no matter what and that is just what I did. I threw the diaper bag together. Grabbed a few just in case things then finished my makeup and we were on our way.

After a brief meeting at the Tottenville High School with Katie and her crew, Lisa said we needed to go to the site where the house was so off we went. The smell of destruction was in the air. It looked like the end of the world. It smelled like death and it actually made my lips numb. The smell was a distinct smell kind of like salt-water, mold, basement, and dirt. The smell was faint but foul smelling enough to notice. When I brought some pictures home from the site every time I would touch them, I could smell it. Even opening the bag I can smell it. When we first got there, Gerard and the girls went down the block chatting with Katie as the camera crew followed. The story was just so riveting Katie herself was teary eyed. It was devastating and surreal.

I was hesitant to venture down the block. I spoke to a

woman that lived down the street she had a heavy

Spanish accent and when I told her who I was; she looked

at me with pity. She said, "I tell George to leave and No

stay there…I say come to my house, but he no listen." I just shook my head lost for words .There are no words to describe the shock and pain I was feeling. My eyes just welled up and I just kept thinking of Angela. I thought of how she was like a lamb lead to the slaughter. I thought of how angry she was that night writing her posts. I told the woman that Gerard also had begged them to get out of there but they refused.

I looked around and saw the destruction further down the road. I simply could not take my eyes off piles of debris everywhere. So much that you could barely park the car because it narrowed the road. Debris piled about fifteen feet high at least and most people who had been there for quite some time wore masks. There were literally hundreds of people trying to help and Police everywhere. They were making sure that if you were there you either lived there or had a purpose. I had seen the absolute worst natural disaster unfold first hand and I was standing with my youngest daughter in tow, right in the thick of its repercussions. I ventured down the road.

When I got there, I revered looking at the people there sacrificing their time and comforts. My jaw just dropped at the sight I saw. There was nothing there but the cement stairs. I took it in and stood there in the moment. I took this picture. The people there were all helping working together as a community. There were some walking around with coffee for everyone and some donating food and serving food to all the volunteers. The people pulled together using all their resources for the good of everyone who was in need. The storm hit them hard and all the people were there with the intent to help. What an impact this made on my life and how I think and what I value now. I see that all of your possessions really in the big picture mean nothing. All you own might be taken from you and just washed away literally or figuratively at any time. Having that knowledge will make you value people. Sometimes we take for granted those fleeting enjoyable moments that you need to stop for a second and absorb.

The house I spent many holidays in was gone. My daughters visited and stayed there with Angela constantly. So many memories all of their things and all that they treasured washed away in the blink of an eye. I saw an old familiar face Cindy. She was a dear friend of Gerard's Sister Carol Ann. Cindy looked at me and gave me a half smile then a big hug from the heart. I have not seen her in about thirteen years but there was a connection unbroken and I could not stop the tears. Groups of Angela's friends were there and they knew my girls. So many pictures were collected from the site.

Cindy and so many of others were there trying to find and salvage any pictures and possessions they could find of Angela's, Patricia's, or Georges. Some findings were worth mentioning and some just sad to see.

These are a few of the treasures. The girls brought them home, washed them, and laid them out to dry. To them they are little bits and pieces of Angela.

Patricia's wedding gown was found hanging in a tree with both arms out like angel wings. My girls walked around the site hoping to find just something to hold onto, little pieces of what looked like garbage to me they picked up and recognized as part of Angela's things and articles from her bedroom and Aunt Patricia's Knick Knacks. So sad I could cry. I held it in until I hit the main road on the way home. I always try to stay strong for my girls no matter what the circumstances but, even writing this now it is very difficult to fight the tears.

A few days before the volunteers got to the site the sanitation workers came and removed the large debris. Gerard went there with his friend Mitch Buchhalter. It was very difficult to look through the rubble. This was his sister's house. The house he went to so he could relax and be comfortable, laugh and enjoy his children and his niece. It was his family time. Now this place was gone his sister is left in the lurch. "How can I go to look at that?"

Gerard said he did not want to go so he went to the area near there and stayed a few blocks away still not yet willing to go see the destruction. Eventually his friend Mitch talked him into it. They went to the site and they started to search. Mitch got down on his hands and knees to dig and found a wedding band that turned out to be George's. He was a plumber and did not wear the wedding band he kept it in a drawer in the kitchen. Jo Ann had said she wanted to go there with a metal detector to see if she could find any jewelry. It is amazing to have it recovered when it could have been lost at sea forever. Nevertheless, Patricia confirmed it was his. They walked around and of all things, Gerard found an old card with his name on it.

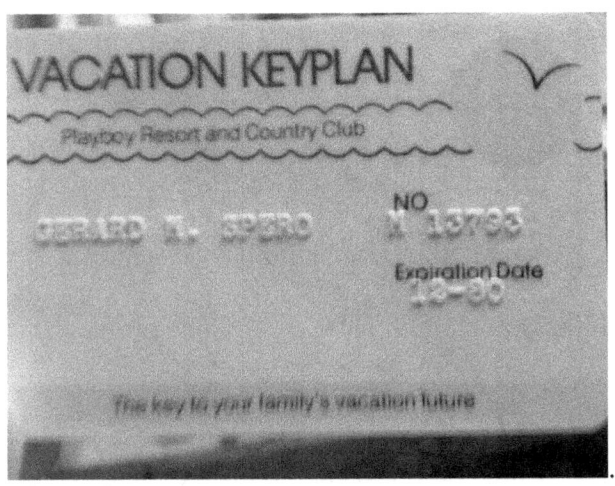

It expired in 1980. As he was looking down at the
wedding band Mitch was showing him he noticed a card
under his shoe and thought it was a credit card so he
picked up. Why in the world Patricia have this, I do not
know. How it wound up under his shoe out of all the
debris, I cannot imagine that. There were so many strange
coincidences and so many peculiar occurrences that made
me believe the fates had their design planned out. I am
not sure what to believe. I tossed ideas around in my head
that maybe; just maybe Angela's fate was this… from the

moment she was born. Maybe my marriage to Gerard could not have worked because then the girls would have never been so close with Angela. I am not sure what I believe and most people are unsure when it comes to fate and afterlife. I know that a few weeks before this storm I had the worst feeling of death surrounding me. So intense that I thought it might be me that was going to die. I told my friend Heather information incase I did die. As soon as the storm hit that feeling went away. I do think that once the man who robbed the Dresch home took action and stole from them during hurricane Irene 2011 this tragedy was destiny. Possibly this was destined for 20 years. The past year seemed to be creating this result and it could not be changed once the course was set. I have a strange ability. The sixth sense you have heard about is the only way I can describe it. Sometimes I wish I didn't but I just know things.

In November of 2008, I got the worst feeling about my cousin Ronny and I was right he had gotten into some trouble. Long story short something that had happened to him in November and I believe sealed his fate. Ronny was killed in a motorcycle accident March 7th, 2010. I think destiny shifts with choice and occurrences and his was sealed from the minute I felt something was wrong. I also predicted that someone would die a few years ago and I told my brother "someone is going to die in three weeks." His reply was "WHO ME?" I laughed and said, "I don't know who! I just know it" Three weeks to the day my moms neighbor Ruth, passed away. Ruth was like a grandmother to me all my life. She very was special. I did her hair for 25 years. Ruth died at age 91. She lived a full long life but I miss her still. She was buried on my birthday. I made a believer out of my brother that is for sure.

I have not told any one this until now but when Angela was here in August, I got the strangest empty feeling from her stare. Angela was sitting across from me on the couch and it was as a hollowness I have only seen twice before, once was my friends mom who was dyeing almost as if she had left her body already. The same feeling was there only I did not recognize it until hind's sight. One other time was a friend's eyes. Michelle, she died of liver disease at age 24.She gave me the same unsure, empty feeling. I have some kind of peace with death, knowing that it is pending, inevitable and planned for your life. Death is the end of the soul's journey. Such a part of life is death and some souls are not meant to stay. Angela was here for a short time but the impact she had on so many lives was limitless. Angela will live on in so many hearts and I only hope that my life is as meaningful. I hope that when people think of her, they realize she did what she needed to on this earth and her soul moved on. I hope that her mother, friends, and classmates all realize she is at peace, moving on to the next phase her soul needs to go through. However, it certainly does not make it any easier, or make anyone miss her less.

Back at home in Brick, a crazy out of season snowstorm had taken over the town. This crazy weather was so out of control, the power was still out and we were not at all prepared for such a storm. It came out of nowhere. The temperature had dropped and the night was closing in. Having the baby made me very concerned about the cold. Even with the heat off and the heaters going by generator, I still could not get the temperature in the baby's room above 60 degrees. The teens were only concerned about the battery life of their phones that seemed to die out even faster in the cold.

At the site, I snapped this picture of Miquela and

Marielle.

This picture is absolutely the hardest one to look at for me. Every time I see it, I think of my daughters searching through the debris so desperate for something to hold onto from Angela. So happy when they would pick up something that they recognized from her room. It was just so sad for me to watch them do that. Some things just wear you down. Our hearts beat and we wake up each morning to a new day. The sun rises and sets life goes on. Our minds are full of memories of the events that stole Angela and George from our lives. For my daughters there is no longer a recollection of the past that they enjoyed with their dad. Their childhood with Angela now is weighed down by the heaviness of grief. I see a glow of laughter when they remember her that quickly fades with the realization of their loss.

We talked to some of Angela's friends there and they knew my girls - one girl handed me four pictures , right on top....and there is no way for her to have known this ,

there was a picture of Carol Ann and Jo Ann standing on
my moms front walk on the day of my wedding to
Gerard.

Now you tell me, do you think that is a coincidence?
Maybe it is but, I believe Carol Ann was there that day
seeing the devastation, feeling the pain and her sprit lead

that girl my way, and she was sent to me so that I would know that. I have heard from spirit in the past but I seldom speak of my interactions and predictions. I have been known to make predictions and communicate with the dead. I do not try to make people understand because they look at me as if I am insane. Usually people do not believe what they cannot see.

Chapter 5

Starfish

There were so many people helping. One woman in
particular, her name is Erin Forrest. I had a detailed
phone interview with Erin. We have been conversing
through email. This woman is just wonderful. She is
constantly selflessly helping. She has been volunteering
as much as she possibly can. She was compelled to keep
helping. You see, she saw the story about Patricia, she
had heard about all the people that needed help. She got
in her car drove to Staten Island from Manhattan looking
to help she drove down Hylan Boulevard not knowing
that it ended in Tottenville. Erin had decided to volunteer
to help. Erin went to Tottenville High School and helped
there first. She drove a family that needed a ride. They
were going to a place they found to stay. She then

randomly turned down Yetman Avenue she saw the destruction and was willing to help. She got to the site and put on some gloves. She saw a girl who seemed to be answering everyone's questions and asked what she could do to help, the girl replied, "You can help pick up and sort through and clean off the dirt. Then just put the things you find in the bins"

 It turns out that someone that she had asked was Jo Ann, Angeles older sister. She saw someone talking to Jo Ann and she realized that this was the story that she had read about in the newspaper. She also saw Gerard and the Girls talking to Katie. Erin realized they were the people in the tragic story that had compelled her to drive there and start helping but she did not know it until then.

This ballerina was found on the day of

the benefit. Jo Ann was looking for it from the first day

that Erin found the male ballerina that inspired her to

have a benefit to raise money for Patricia.

As she combed the beach looking for items to gather, clean, and restore she came across a broken porcelain male ballerina figurine. Erin is a dance instructor, and now it all made sense to her. Erin spoke to the owner of the dance studio where she works in Manhattan. His name is Edward Ellison. He had come up with the idea to have a fundraiser to raise money for Patricia to rebuild her life. He had said that he wanted to do the fundraiser but give the money to the Red Cross however; Erin wanted to put a face to their efforts and know exactly where that money was going. She saw firsthand the destruction, heard the horrible story, and wanted the fundraiser to be for Patricia. Erin had asked me, "Did you ever hear the story about the starfish?" I said "no" so she continued, "There was a little girl who walked along the beach and she wanted to save the starfish that were washed ashore so she picked one up and threw it into the ocean. A man saw her and asked why you are doing that you cannot save them all. The girl replied "But I did save that one." This story (or maybe a little angel on Erin's shoulder) told her she could just save one. Lucky for Patricia she was that one little starfish.

The same day the event was held there was also a soccer game played as a benefit. They called it "Playing for Angels" The angels that they are referring to are Angela and George.

Gerard and the girls stopped by to thank them in the early afternoon. They only stayed for a short time and then went to get ready for the ballet fundraiser.

Strangely, on the day I was writing about the soccer

game the SI Advance had an article about it! This picture

was taken over the summer 2012.

Chapter 6

The Unsung Heroes

Edward Ellison and Erin Forrest decided to have a ballet benefit in Manhattan on Saturday, December 8th at 8 PM 2012. Because of Erin, all proceeds from show will go to the "Dresch family fund" that Gerard had set up before the Katie Couric show. Erin is truly a hero. There are few people with the time to do all that she does. There are even fewer people with the heart and energy, not to mention the gumption to take the initiative to get it done! She is constantly working to help. Erin truly cares for others, and she keeps doing all that she can...

Gerard is a hero. He saved his sister's life by making the call to 911 and sitting on hold for almost an hour. What's more, he tried to prevent Angela and George's deaths. Gerard told them to leave, he begged them to leave, but they stayed. Gerard was there for Patricia and identified the bodies and he and Jo Ann, Patricia's older daughter, planned the funerals. They both did that and much more. Jo Ann is also a hero. She and her husband Brad came from Tennessee. They drove to Staten Island and immediately started helping to salvage what she could from the site where the house was. She cleaned and sorted everything found.

My girls Miquela and Marielle are heroes simply because they stood strong. They are fourteen and fifteen, a difficult age without something like this happening. They are making sure everyday that Angela's memory is kept the way Angela would have wanted it to be. Along with Angela's Best friend Kat and a few others, they defend Angela's honor if needed now when #AngelAngela isn't here to defend herself. They monitor Facebook, Instagram, and Twitter and make sure her memory is left unscathed everyday. They miss her everyday.

Gerard and the girls and Jo Ann attended the Ballet benefit. Before the show started the seven-minute segment that aired on the Katie Couric show began, when it was over they went out on the stage to thank everyone for his or her support. They also sold the bracelets there we had made up for donations. It is amazing what two hands can do. The one woman that put herself out there offered her time and energy resulted in so many contributing. She just wanted to be helpful and it did wonders. Erin made such a difference. Erin Forrest is a hero. When we spoke I told her that I had not seen too much of that. Someone who did not just help, however, she collaborated with the dance school owner to have an event including many people to help, all for Patricia. She is a beautiful soul. I am looking forward to meeting her someday. This is sort of a mini chapter kind of a tribute to these people who worked, helped, grieved, and never had a selfish intention. I cannot hold back the tears writing this chapter. My hope is that they read this and all know how proud I am of them. I want them to know their love and support did not go unnoticed.

Chapter 7

Just doing our part

It was amazing to see the outpour of volunteers and their love they are at the site that day. It inspired us to do something to help. These are the bracelets that the girls and I decided to create to do our part in helping raise money for "Aunt P" (as they call her) we made up bracelets in Angela's honor. Every bracelet that we sent out, I wrote a note on the back of every envelope thanking them for supporting us.

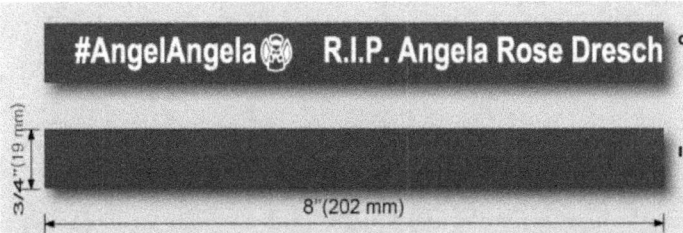

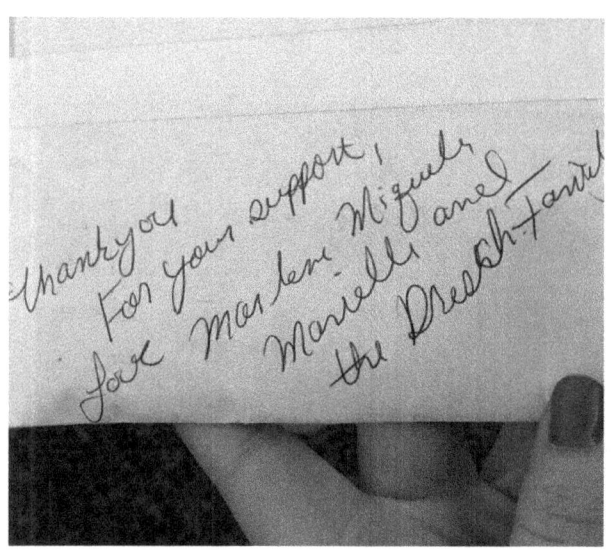

Out of four hundred bracelets, we managed to sell approximately 350. My head and my heart are heavy even being somewhat distanced from the devastation. I am still shocked, heart broken, and changed forever. It is amazing the experience of the storm and walking on the site seeing what I have seen. The destruction was certainly a site that you never quite get out of your head.

A Darkroom, cold air and a flashlight suddenly I am back to that storm with the power out, hearing about Angela and George in disbelief.

Chapter 8

The moon, the fire, and Katie

It's a full moon today its beautiful but, I am writing

today 11/29/12 10:39pm one month later and I am trying

to wrap my head around it still .Forever …the full moon

will hold the memory of this event and Angela and her

very short life. The storms, and of course Halloween

holds a haunting memory of hearing about George's body

being found. I'm staring at the lit fire in the fireplace

thinking; I feel like a part of me died –something inside

that made me feel I would live forever is now certainly

gone. There was a part of me that felt the system, the

government, nature, the whole world was formatted and I

was safe. I do not feel safe anymore. I do not think that I

will ever be the same. It took so long for the system to

recover and get power to the residents in some areas it

was out for weeks. Maybe it really is the end of the world.

Since she was discharged from the hospital, Patricia is staying in a house that is next to the church where she works teaching CCD classes. She returned to work in early December. The house is owned by the church and she needs to be out by March. How fortunate that she has this place to stay. The funerals alone were so costly. We are hoping the Katie show can help raise money, because she mentioned the fund "The Dresch Family Fund" in TD Bank.

Gerard and the girls stayed at the site much longer than I did. The girls stayed in NY because they were going to be on the Katie show the next day. Miquela had said to me "I just want to stay, and look for more of Angela's things" They were staying in the city and a limo came to pick them up, it was a great distraction for them, Gerard, and Jo Ann. The four of them are all so grief stricken and overwhelmed with this. It was good for them to go to take their minds off their loss for the time being. The show was filmed in the morning on the day it aired Monday November 5th 2012 at 3:00pm I posted and tweeted and everyone who knew us tuned in. In fact, the girls got somewhat famous from the whole tragedy. The Katie show was a tearjerker and had such an impact when you watched it. The girls composed themselves well. Jo Ann was well spoken and Gerard did most of the talking as usual. As the pictures were shown to the audience, they showed the people watching. There were so many people in the audience crying. Jon Bon Jovi was on the show the same day talking about his soup kitchen. He posed for a picture with them, another welcomed distraction.

Once the filming of the show was over and it aired,

reality was back in our faces. The storm affected NJ so

badly in our area. Halloween fun and trick-or-treating

was postponed in our neighborhood. Therefore, while the

girls were still on their way home from filming show, my

husband and I tried to take Mariah trick-or-treating but

that was an epic fail! She cried until we brought her home. The girls did not go this year. They did buy costumes before the tragedy but there was too much going on. Now Halloween and its meaning is something very different for us. As the time passed the funeral plans were being made the strangest things that had happened over the last week started coming to light, as if the wedding dress spread out like angel wings wasn't enough. There were rosary beads draped though the trees as well. Patricia is very religious, staying true to her faith throughout her life. It is no surprise that she had rosary beads all around the house but it is bizarre they were hanging like that. While she was in the hospital, Cardinal

Dolan came to visit her and brought her new rosary

beads.

This picture was taken on New Years Eve 2012 after

midnight mass.

The little purple bear story is very interesting. We found

out that the night of the storm a bear Angela had given to

Sister Maryann Michael when she was four years old had fallen off the shelf. The bear sat on the shelf for all these years. Angela would always ask her if she still had it, because Sister Michael would always give things away. The night of the storm it fell from the shelf, she realized it was time to give it away. The next morning she heard that Patricia was in the hospital. Sister Michael did not know that Angela had passed away, no one did. As soon as we found out, the only conclusion was Angel Angela was sending a sign that it was now time to give the bear away to her mom. She will treasure it forever.

Chapter 9

Respects

On the day of the wakes for Angela and her dad, the girls and I got ready and off we went to Grammy house to leave Mariah because my husband Michael worked nights and was in a deep sleep. My parents gladly watched her and the three of us went to Staten Island to view and pay our last respects. There were so many familiar faces as we brought the huge picture collage of the girls and Angela into the funeral parlor. Miquela and Marielle spent hours creating it. It reads "Cousins by Blood Friends by Choice" The conversations about Angela in our house are constant. We feel her presence with us today and in our home everyday.

The wake was the saddest day I can remember for the girls and I. Surely for Patricia, Gerard and the rest of the family as well. I could not believe that someone reached out to "The Iconic boys" the girls were so obsessed with a year earlier, and waited on line to see. Nick Mara one of Angela's favorites had come to the wake. I was actually relieved because as soon as we got there Miquela was visibly shaken and could not walk up to the coffins and sat down with Gerard's girlfriend Vicki. Marielle and I walked up. The coffin was small and white and she looked peaceful. George did not look like himself. I noticed that he had on an Elvis tee shirt, and it sparked a tear of past laughs with him when I was married to Gerard. It was hard to look at him and imaging the laughs we had. I stood before them still in disbelief. I went to hug Patricia said "She always liked you" and the grief hit me, the tears hit me, our history and connection was there. She hugged me and sobbed. It was very sad. I returned to my older daughter and thanked Vicki for being there as a distraction. She is like the other me I wish I had. We went to show one of Vicki's friend's kids the enormous poster board the girls made and that is when we found out that Nick Mara had come. We walked up to him as he went to pay his respects to one of his biggest fans Angela Rose. It was so nice of him and a great detraction for Miquela as well. She would not go up to see Angela and George until Nick had arrived and made her feel better. Then the chatter began and Camille, Gerard's cousin came to get the girls to meet one of the firefighters who saved Patricia's life. He was also at the wake while I was there. We got the chance to meet him. We were talking to Nick with the girls and everyone felt a little better.

As it turns out Gerard had called the Police station to thank them for sending Marc to the wake. However, they never contacted him. He had come to see Patricia on his own.

So many people came to the wake on Saturday evening and all day Sunday, the line went all the way out the door. Angela was very well liked and most of her classmates came to pay their respects. In addition, any and all who knew George. The media did not let up though. They showed up for the funeral and spoke with classmates of Angela's. Her classmates stood along the walkway in front of the school she attended. Hundreds of them were filmed standing with their hands over their hearts as the hearse passed by.

This all seems surreal.

This candid picture speaks a thousand words.

On the side of the school, a man named Scott LoBaido painted this Flag and in the center of the medallion put, Angela's initials AD. This is him pictured with the

Principal of IS34 along with Patricia.

The girls working on the poster board with 240 pictures

of them over the past 13 years. Making sure the memories

of Angela live on.

Sometimes the closest people to you are the ones who have the toughest jobs. As I said in my tribute Chapter 6 "Unsung Heroes" Jo Ann, Patricia's older daughter not only drove here from Tennessee, and helped with gathering pieces of what was left from the site where the house was. She even washed out cash that was found and dried it. She helped restore the pictures salvaged. Anything she could do she did. Jo Ann was there for her as soon as she possibly could be and she carried her self-well through the whole ordeal. Jo Ann stood by her mother's side and helped her the entire time she was in N.Y. Gerard and Jo Ann along with her husband Brad all three in my opinion are to be commended for all they have done to help Patricia. Sometimes the people closest to you are the ones you forget to thank. So remember to thank those who do the most for you. Gerard called 911... If he did not call there would not have been anyone looking for them that night. Although his efforts were in vein, he did all he could. Remember Gerard, Patricia's brother, Jo Ann, her surviving daughter, also Edward and Erin the kindest strangers. Remember Miquela and Marielle Patricia's nieces and Angela's Best friend Kat. These are the people I decided I would mention for their dedication to the family. Thanks for selfless efforts, love, and endless support.

Chapter 10

Uncertain future

The firefighters Marc Thalheimer along with five other firemen pulled Patricia from the debris, and saved her. They are definitely heroes, and we cannot thank them enough. Marc stood by her side through this entire ordeal.

Patricia's spirits were still high after losing her home, her husband and daughter to Sandy Storm. Patricia was so thankful to the people in her community and her friends who helped her find a place to stay. She was very lucky she had no broken bones but she looked like she was beat up when she arrived at the hospital. The scars inside will never heal.

Patricia never returned to the site where the house once stood, she said she would never go down there again. At one time Patricia loved the beach and now she says that she never wants to go by the water again.

She received many donations. She wrote a letter to the Staten Island advance newspaper to express her heartfelt gratitude. She believes that was the only way to reach every person, since there were so many who had helped her. From the firefighters who saved her to the people who covered her body with warm blankets in the hospital.

There were strangers making donations and she was very grateful. She thought Angela's schoolmates made a beautiful gesture of holding their hands over their hearts as they stood by the school and the hearse drove by.

Still, the future is very uncertain for Patricia even with donations and the outpour of support. The future is unimaginable for her to think of living without her family. Although all her physical injuries have healed, she still has nightmares of being pummeled by the waves and debris. She is also thankful for the little things found in the debris. Just like Miquela and Marielle, she was happy just to have little pieces of things that reminded her of Angela and George, treasures like George's wedding ring. Patricia and George were together since she was 18 years old.

Someone also had found a bracelet that Angela made for her; these are the things she holds close to her heart.

The holidays were especially difficult for her. To Patricia, faith is a very important part of getting through each day. Someday she would like to reach out to other people who lost children or their spouse in Sandy storm 2012. That is very important to her.

❖

❖

Chapter 11

Whisper

During this whole ordeal, I had a dream of Angela. I could only see her face and blackness surrounded her. I heard her say quietly "Thank you, tell her thank you." but, all I could think was… thank you for what? Tell whom? Its strange how as soon as I text Gerard to tell him about the dream the word "Doll" popped in my head and for a second. I though of a real doll like one that a child would have. Then it occurred to me that Angela's Grandparents are both deceased and her grandfather Pasqual Spero called Gerard's mom "Doll"

It seems to make sense to me now. Angela wanted to thank Patricia for trying so hard to save her. It was the most difficult thing to do I'm sure, knowing that your daughter's life was in jeopardy trying to comfort her when she was petrified. Maybe her Grandma is looking out for her now and was there to greet her and George in their passing. Possibly, Doll is here making sure everything is ok with Patricia. Angela's quiet whisper to me was saying that she wanted me to relay that thank you from her to her mom. I am not sure if it was a message from Gerard's father or George telling me about Doll. I know that it was a male voice and with a familiar feel. When I hear these messages, I feel honored to be able to do it. Now that I have had the opportunity to think about it, I am glad who ever it was contacted me.

When I asked Gerard if he asked her about it, he replied, "It's too painful, she doesn't want to talk about it." I hope Patricia reads this and feels good that Angela appreciated what she did for her. I am hoping to find out someday if my strange communications with the spirit world were accurate.

This is the last picture taken of Angela. A "selfie" as my girls call it. Meaning she took a picture of her self. It was taken on the beach by her house just a few hours before she died. I just know it was Angela that I heard the other night. She whispered to me when the chills came over me and I heard "Sandy come at me" in a soft female voice that sounded just like hers. I was trying to think of a title for this book. If it was you, Thanks Ang.

This was the picture and this is where the name of the book came from. The last words from the sweetest girl, and the quiet whisper that told me.

Maybe that is her now a quiet little whisper. The voice

that is whispering to the heroes like Marc, Edward, and

Erin. Making sure Patricia, Gerard, and Jo Ann know she

is happy on the other side and not to feel bad. She is saying to Miquela, Marielle and Kat; please know that I love you and miss you too. She is thanking them for keeping her memory alive. Katherine Hrzic is always posting beautiful pictures of happier times and saying wonderful things about Angela. She has a great picture she has as her cover photo on Facebook of herself, Angela, Marielle, and Miquela taken on the last night they spent with Angela.

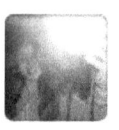

freschtodresch
#COMEATMESANDY

miqueque
did you have to leave your house?!?

freschtodresch
nah my mom said were not leaving but if
we have to I'm gunna live in my car

miqueque
lololololol

This was the conversation between Miquela and Angela

the night of the storm.

127

Chapter 12

Someday, I will

Miquela wrote a story about Angela for dance class and she got a 100 on it! I had spoken with her guidance councilor and she told me that she was going to inform all her teachers of the tragedy and she did not. When I read what the teacher wrote about her work, and the tragedy, that was confirming to me that it does not matter if you knew Angela. It does not matter if you are young or old. Everyone who hears about this story is impacted. The story and its details are so implausible. Knowing the family for 20 years and having the inside scoop of everything that took place that night of the storm, makes me realize it CAN happen. It is so difficult to understand knowing Angela and what she loved and dreamed for the future. It is even harder to except knowing the things that she shared with her closest friends- my daughters; it makes it so much more painful. I hope to make people realize that if you are told to evacuate usually it is for a good reason and the precautions should be taken seriously.

My life has been like a crazy ride and I have told the strangest stories and heard repeatedly 'Marlene you should write a book!' I have considered writing about topics I was interested in. I thought maybe I would write about things that had happened to me but nothing inspired me. Then the storm and destruction made such an impact on my life and the deaths of Angela and George weighed heavy on my heart so much I could not stop typing. I knew this was the someday I waited for and this was the story I would write. This is a story like no other. I always said, "Someday I will, I'll write a book when I have a story that needs to be to be told." I am also now inspired to write about other true incredible stories as well.

Chapter 13

Memoires

I have remarried and love my new family however; I still consider The Spero and Dresch families my family as well and that will never change. That is why I am so distraught over this tragedy. All the time and space between me and the people that I love disappears. Some have grown, married, and moved on with their lives. Some just moved. There are some I just lost touch with and of course those who passed away. Although there is pain in my heart and an indescribable emptiness that cannot be filled, there is one thing that time and distance cannot take away. No one can ever take the one thing I have and that is all the memories of the love and happiness. Memories I will have and treasure forever.

Chapter 14

#AngelAngela Pictures -Never forgotten

Angela took this on her phone and sent it to me of her

and Mariah.

Angela's own collage

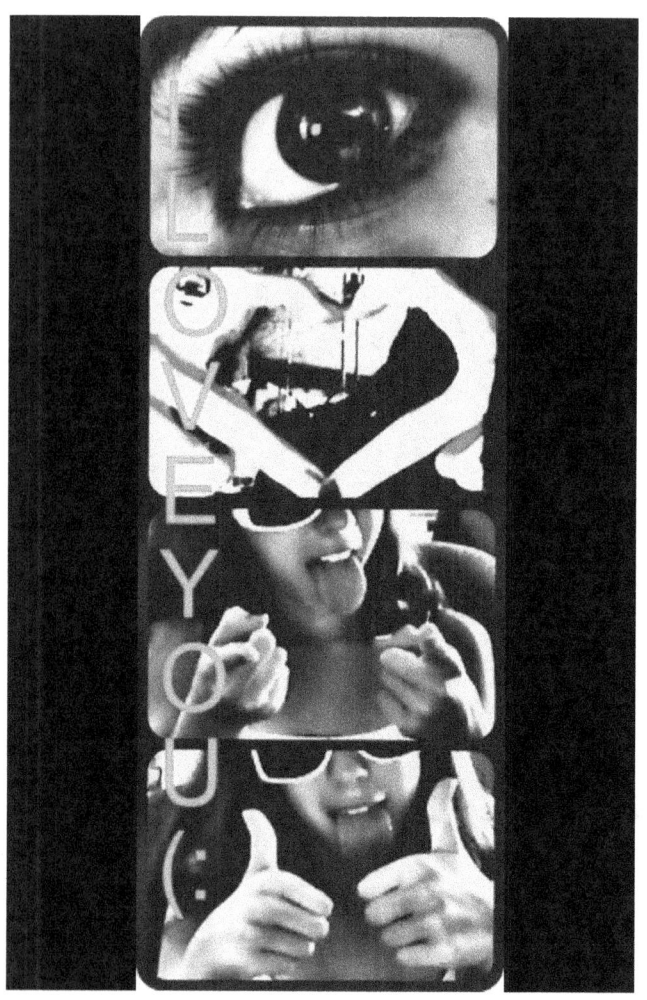

Diabetes walk October 14, 2012

Growing up together

My mom Maxine Kuzma, Angela, Marielle, Me, and

Miquela at Miquela's Dance Recital 2011

The previous pictures are special. The first one is of Angela and her sister Jo Ann I hijacked it from Jo Ann's pictures on Facebook. The one below was a Santa picture but not just Angela on any random Santa's lap .It is one of the pictures handed to me at the site of the house that day. It is also special because every year George dressed up as Santa and this is actually a picture of George holding Angela.

This past spring 2012 we would wind up have lunch

together for the first time in about thirteen years. We had

a really bad waiter, but the kids got free milkshakes!

This is Angela 10 months old with her Grandfather

Gerard's father Pasquale Spero.

Angela Rose ... ♡

Top: Gerard and the girls at the beach

Bottom: Gerard's Sister Carol Ann holding Angela with her friend

Connie and Miquela next to them on the right.

Done

Happy Father's Day! I love you Daddy!!!
xoxoxo

6 Likes

This was a post from Father's day 2012. Hijacked from

Angela's pictures!

Top picture was the girls at Great Adventure. The last

time I saw Angela she stayed at our house and they went

to Great Adventure with my husband. I am so glad that

Michael has gotten to know her. I am so glad that the last

time she stayed with us they had such great time.

RIP George Dresch 8/1/1957-10/31/2012

George was known as the person to go to if you needed help. He could fix things. He was always helping out doing things for others. George Dresch, beloved father and husband. I knew him as a brother-in-law who was always joking around. He knew the girls liked him and he always was kidding around calling them mouse's. He was a fun Uncle. He was a devoted family man. George, you will be missed.

Angela posted this picture of herself and she looked so
pretty I could not resist adding it to the book.

This is Angela's eighth grade graduation picture. She never got to see it. They were given out at her wake.

R.I.P.Angela Rose Dresch 4/30/1999-10/29/2012

Believe

Believe that disaster can happen to you. Believe you can

survive. Believe it can change you and those people

connected to you. Believe in the spirit world and God.

Believe in miracles, fate, and destiny......

Six months after the storm I speak to Patricia almost every day now and we have finally become close after 21 years. Even when I was married to her brother Gerard, we were not close because Patricia does not drive and I worked in New Jersey. Within one year I was pregnant and for the next three years of our marriage practically! And had two daughters 19 months apart. I was extremely busy. Gerard's older sister Carol Ann and her friend Connie lived around the corner and dropped by quite often to see the girls so her and I were very close. After we got divorced in 2002, Patricia and I rarely spoke. My daughters Miquela and Marielle were always there at the house with Angela and very close to the family. A disaster that tore the family apart and killed her husband and her youngest daughter Angela has changed her inside and out. It defines her now, changing her life forever. She will always be a survivor, but always be in pain from it. However, I believe good things will come from it. We gained a friendship from it and that is just the beginning.

Patricia became close with the one firefighter that had caught a glimpse of a light that led to her rescue. She has a special bond with him. Five months after the storm I finally spoke to her and gave her pictures, I had of Angela. The past month has been very strange for both of us; I will try to explain where some peculiar happenings begin.

Patricia had gone to a medium, and she had told Miquela and Marielle what the medium had told her. The girls were shocked when it was exactly what I had said five months earlier. I had told Gerard to tell Patricia about my dream that Angela was saying thank you and wanted her to know that she appreciated that she had tried to save her. I also told her I heard a male voice tell me specifically that "Doll" was there to meet them when they crossed over that night. I guess, hearing this exact information from two people she came to a turning point and a realization of the spirit world. From that moment on Patricia and I had become the best of friends that we should of been for 21 years. This began more interactions with the spirit world and opened the door for so many spirits to connect with people on earth that cannot hear them. A few weeks after I heard that word "doll" I was kneeling in the bathroom giving my youngest daughter Mariah a bath and I had a flash of a young man with brown hair next to her smiling at the same time I heard

'it's in the change or in the coins'. My messages are

always jumbled up. I didn't understand if it was saying in

the coins or by the coins, I just understood he was

relating to me "the change and the coins". Being the male

figure flashed in my head, I thought it was my cousin

Ronny who passed away three years earlier in a

motorcycle accident. I told my aunt Edna (who is his

mom) to check in his change and coins if he had any.

Being a nonbeliever, she brushed off what I had said. I

kept hounding her because I believed it was a message.

As it turns out it was but, not for my aunt Edna. This

message was for Patricia from her late husband George.

Shortly after I started talking to Patricia, I found out that she had not yet looked through the things that were recovered at the site where the house was. I could not believe that her curiosity wasn't peaked! I told her to look in there and I did not know why I felt she needed to. She asked me to do it with her and then she would. I believed she should go through the process before she moves into a new home and starts fresh. When the very first thing we found was a bag that had not been there before and everything inside was very dirty and it just so happens that it was filled with George's change and coins then I knew. There were a few pictures in there also one was Angela and Patricia's mom another of George. As soon as she opened the bag, she said "oh! That's George's change and his coins" Miquela immediately turned to look at me. I just said "no way!" I had the chills over my entire body! "The change and coins" was an accurate message but I did not recognize whom the message was from or whom it was for. I know now why I was compelled to go and help Patricia go through the things recovered. Apparently, the message was George telling Patricia to go get them. There were some things in there that had made her cry and some things that weren't even hers! However, she was very glad she started the difficult process.

I kept hearing "God is moving mountains for me." One night I was talking to Patricia telling her this and that I believed that our lives were connected somehow now. We hung up and she text me telling me that that line was in George's song. A song that every time she heard it, it reminded her of him. I said to her "what God is moving mountains?" She said, "Yes ma'am." Just at that exact moment, the song came on the radio. Patricia called me back and cried and said "what is going on!?" She sobbed and said, "what is this?"

Now that I understand better how to determine when I hear messages, it seems they are coming through more often. I have spirit coming to me that I do not even know that are connected to people in my life. I started hearing from many different spirits on a daily basis. Sometimes I do not know who the messages are for. What People in my life the sprits want to help or connect with. Most of the spirits contact me through my dreams. It is in the last five seconds of my sleep messages come through

sometimes it is in like half sleep twilight. I know I am

sleeping and seeing clearly but it is not a dream. It is a

message from spirit. I get very frustrated when all my

messages are so jumbled up. I wonder if it's because my

life is so busy and my thoughts are jumbled up. I chuckle

and wonder if it's just because my talent as a medium is

lacking. Although as I have said, since everything

happened with Patricia and Angela and George contacted

me I had stranger spirits contacting me. I have never met

my old roommate's former partner Claire. She passed

away while she was partners in owning and running a

salon with my former roommate Linda. The message was

distinctly from her telling Linda that she must attend the

meeting. She definitely believed that the meeting was

crucial for Linda to attend. When I relayed this message back to Linda she informed me that a meeting was coming up with her landlord and current partner about the money that she stole from Linda and why she did not pay the rent. Please make sure you make that meeting! I also told her that Claire was very clear on that.

In between chit chatting with Patricia, running the girls around, and my crazy baby that I am trying to potty train, I keep having interactions with the spirit. I do not think many people believe me unless they experience it firsthand and get an accurate reading.

It seems whenever I speak to Patricia strange things happen like a song that means something to her or reminds her of George or Angela comes on the radio. I was talking to her on the phone on Wednesday April 24, 2013 it was very late night. She was going through her pocketbook preparing for her trip to Washington. We were talking about finding the bag of coins and my premonition. We were talking about spirits and Angela. We talked about things being out of your control. She was switching bags and reached in to the pocketbook she has been using all winter. She was surprised when she found a box with rosary beads she exclaimed "what is this, where did it come from?" There was also a coin in the box that had the serenity prayer on it and a bear that said "one day at a time". Patricia said she never saw it before in her life! This was all the things we were talking about in one box. She said, "How could I have been carrying this around all winter and not have found it?" I told her that she was supposed to find it at that moment so it could confirm to her again that she was hearing from the spirit world, more importantly Angela and George. They are letting her know they hear her and love her.

Moving on

Thursday, April 25, 2013

I just spoke to Patricia she told me she met with Michael

Grimm and had an interview in New York. The

government is doing a buyout program and Patricia is

fortunate enough to be the very first person on the list of

people to receive a check for the home she lost. This was

great news to make a fresh start. Although she still will

need money to fill the home with furniture.

She took a train to Washington. She had a great time and

she said it was just a wonderful experience.

This is Patricia with Michael Grimm

So many people have helped her. She has met amazing

people over the past six months.

Then on Friday, April 26, she finally met the other five

firefighters that saved her. She finally met all of them.

They told her they were very unsure walking over the

debris from the roofs of houses to get her. They feared

that it would collapse or they would fall into someone's

pool. As they walked, they poked with a stick to see if it

was solid enough to step on. Before this she only met and

spoke to Mark the one firefighter that came to the

funerals. They took many pictures; here are a few candid

shots. They may be in the newspaper with an article in

the Staten Island advance newspaper.

Monday, April 29, 2013

Patricia was interviewed by CNN about the tragedy and

the past six months. She has shared with me how much

she is afraid of moving forward and at the same time how

much she cannot wait to set up house again. She lives in the house next to the church still, and she does not have a TV or Internet access. She does not decorate or feel at home there. She wants to bake again. She will not even sleep upstairs in the bedroom she sleeps downstairs on the couch. I read this chapter to her, to get her seal of approval and I got many tears. All she could say when I got to this part about her setting up house again was that Angela and George won't be there. She cried so much she had to hang up.

On Tuesday, April 30, 2013, a mass was held for Angela. It would have been her 14th birthday. It is a very sad day for Patricia, Angela's friends and the whole family.

Patricia also would love to do a follow-up on the Katie show. She wants to connect with other people who have lost loved ones in Sandy storm 2012. Although she is going to counseling and a bereavement group, it is hard for her to connect with them because their circumstances were all different. She feels that for her to connect, grieve, and feel better about what has happened she needs to speak with them. There was one woman who lost two children. She reached out to her and hopes to connect with her soon. I believe that Patricia will make a difference to this woman, to society and to the world. She is strong and was saved for a reason, now she is on a journey to find out what it is.

A portion of the proceeds from this book will go to the Dresch family fund. Here is information if you wish to contribute more. A sincere thank you, all donations are greatly appreciated.

Please make checks payable to:

Dresch Family Fund

c/o TD Bank

126 Page Avenue

Staten Island N.Y.

10309

.

www.ingramcontent.com/pod-product-compliance
Lightning Source LLC
Chambersburg PA
CBHW070650290526
45790CB00001B/259